T0114891

# Other books by Author

... more will be revealed ...

# WAR WITHIN

## WW VIII:
## My Mental State

# MICHAEL R. BANE

WESTBOW
PRESS®
A DIVISION OF THOMAS NELSON
& ZONDERVAN

WestBow Press books may be ordered through booksellers or by contacting:

WestBow Press
A Division of Thomas Nelson & Zondervan
1663 Liberty Drive
Bloomington, IN 47403
www.westbowpress.com
844-714-3454

Scripture quotations marked KJV are taken from the King James Version.

ISBN: 979-8-3850-1637-2 (sc)
ISBN: 979-8-3850-1638-9 (e)

Library of Congress Control Number: 2024901155

Print information available on the last page.

WestBow Press rev. date: 1/23/2024

# CONTENTS

## Chapter 1   Addiction

## Chapter 2   Anxiety

## Chapter 3   Autism

## Chapter 4   Bipolar

## Chapter 5   Borderline Personality Disorder

## Chapter 6   Depression

## Chapter 7   Dissociative Idenity Disorder (DID)

## Chapter 8   Panic

## Chapter 9   PTSD

# Chapter 10 Schizophrenia

# Chapter 11 Self Injury/Cutting

# INTRO

## My Mental State

My mental health is a huge part of my story. In the continuation of this series (War Within).

It would not be complete if I did not at least attempt to include this in my writings.

I invite you into my mind
as well as into my journey.

# - DEDICATION -

## My Mental State

I dedicate this edition WW VIII to Barbara Ann. You know who you are. I'm just not sure if you know how special you are to me.

Giving me your support, and love.

And taking the time to actually read, and get involved in my life.

I'm so grateful that God brought us together.

# PREFACE 1

## - Self Medication -

I'm going to attempt to address some of the mental conditions, or disorders known to me, and to so many others.

First; I must say that I am in no way a proffessional in any of these areas.

But through my life experiences over the years, I have had many of these symptoms, and behaviors.

Poetry seems to be my greatest therapy.

The way I communicate best, is through my poems.

So I will attempt to express my thoughts, and ideas in that way

Many of the poems were written over the years.

Also, I am writing more now to try to touch on as many of these conditions that I can.

A little bit about me.

I was inthrawled in my addiction to drugs, and alcohol for many, many years.

And looking back I see how I may have been self medicating my whole life.

I was 40 years old, when I finally got clean.

It was a long journey, and it truly is a miracle that I made it out alive.

I'm one of the few.

The lines that I crossed, I can never safely go back.

For people like me, thier are only 3 ways out;

Life in prison, death, or recovery.

And I thank God, my Lord, and Savior that He chose me to recover.

Thier was many attempts at recovery, but it never lasted for more than a few months.

I'm gonna throw out a few numbers, they are not exact, but the best estimation, or educated guess that I can.

From the time I was 20 until I finally got clean at 40. I was arrested over 50 times. In jails all over the country including prison.

I was in mental health, or behavioral health wards 3 times.

Approximately 12 rehabs for addiction, also a minimum of 4 half-way houses, which was a part of the rehab long term care process.

To make a long story short. I was doing life on the installment plan.

I honestly believe that each arrest, and each hospital visit was God's way of saving me from myself.

I used to call it "being in my cage".

And I thought it was the only way I could stay clean.

I truly believe thier are many people out there who are like me. Who may be self medicating with alcohol, and a variety of street drugs.

For many of us their may be an underlying mental health condition, or diagnosis.

I, myself was diagnosed with a combination, in which I truly do not remember exactly which ones.

I do remember I was on 5 mental health meds for several years when I first got in recovery.

And over time with Dr.s, and councilors help, I weened off each.

They were so helpful in my early recovery.

I completely believe my recovery, and my mental health go hand in hand.

They must both be treated.

And I cannot do it alone.

So many doctors, councilors, legal professionals, and self-help groups, and programs were a huge part of my recovery.

But my biggest help was God.

Without God in my life, I would be dead, or in prison.

I truly believe this.

Another part of my story was homelessness, or at best, I was couch surfing, laying my head where ever I could.

So as I attempt to express my thoughts, and feelings through my stories, and my poems. Please try not to compare, but try moreso to relate.

I found in life,

that we are more alike than we are different.

# PREFACE 2

## - Simply Complex -

Wow, so as I continue this journey of the mind, and mental health.

I am seeing that I fit in so many of these categories.

It amazes me how complex the mind truly is, and at the same time how simple thoughts, and ideas can make it possible; in many situations for us to take back some control.

Please do not take that last statement out of context.

Each person, and each case is different.

I guess one of my biggest hopes in these writings, is that someone, anyone will realize perhaps for the first time.

That we are not alone.

We are not some kind of creeps, and we have great potential.

You are special, and you are worth great things.

In the following pages I will be sharing some of my experiences, in my journey, and my life.

Poetry seems to be my favorite way of expression.

In my writings, I try to include:

What it was like, what happened, and how it is now.

My poems often have multiple messages

I hope the right person, finds the right poem for them.

I also include bible verses, and references, as God is the biggest part of my recovery, and life.

Without God I am nothing, and with God all things are possible.

# PREFACE 3

## - Order of things -

I chose to do the chapters in alphabetical order.
I do not see one as more, or less than others.
I do see more of me in some, and less in others.
But each has touched me in my life to some degree.

I also decided not to include the clinical symptoms, or behaviors, as there are many, and not everyone agrees on them.

If you see yourself within these pages, you are not alone.

# CHAPTER 1

## ADDICTION

I Peter 5:8

Be sober, be vigilent; because your adversary the devil, as a roaring lion, walketh about, seeking whome he may devour.

KJV

There are many different thoughts, ideas, theories, and reasons for addiction.

So I will share how I kinda define addiction.
If the use of something causes negative results in any area of my life which includes, but not limited to;
physical, mental, emotional, spiritual, social, or legal.

There may be an issue also if I want, or need more of something to obtain previous feelings, or affects I may be addicted.

The most important part that I would like to share about addiction; is that their is a solution.

We don't need to stay where we are, and we don't need to die from the horrors of addiction.

# WHEN IT WAS WRITTEN

# AS A WOLF

The disease of addiction is as a wolf.
A wolf in sheeps clothing.
The wolf is sneaky, sly, and patient.
He sits and waits, he is on the hunt
lulling you to think everythings ok.
Always looking for something, someone to devour.
He gnashes his teeth, and will pick your bones clean and leave nothing but dust that
returns to the earth.
But our spirit he cannot touch.
It returns to God, only if we are His, and He is ours
the wolf lives and breathes death.
the gnarling, the foaming of the mouth
and death lives in him.
We must recognize his camoflage.
We must understand his ways, in order to survive.
The disease of addiction is as a wolf.
A wolf that never dies.

# DOPE FEIN MOVE

I saw an old friend
the other day

But when he saw me
he looked away

His skin was yellow
his hair was gray

His lips were burnt
his clothes were stained

He finally asked me
where I've been

And I told him
I found a new way to live

I asked him to come
I told him its free

I couldn't believe it
when he turned from me

And he said I'm sorry,
I have some place to be

And I thanked God
that was no longer me...

# ME, MY MURDERER

So many people cry
So many people die
this is war
Me, my murderer
I kill myself by my mistakes
by the drugs I take
It was not always this way
I am to blame
this is a war, I cannot win
I kill myself
me, my murderer
So many people die
So many people cry
If you are not like me,
you can not understand these things
the lives it changed
and the pain it brings
by my mistakes
by the drugs I take
So many lives changed
So many lives rearranged
You if you are not like me,
You can not understand such things
But you can understand
The pain it brings
By my mistakes
by the drugs I take
I kill myself
me, my murderer
So many people cry...

# CHAPTER 2

# ANXIETY

Philippians 4:6

Be careful for nothing; but in everything by prayer and supplication with thanksgiving let your requests be made known unto God

KJV

I remember not very long ago,
literally a few weeks back.
I was shopping with a friend of mine
in a large department store.
Unknowingly why I started getting certain feelings.
I will try to explain those feelings now.
I felt like I was trapped, like
I hade to get out of there.
Their was way too much going on,
and I was stressing out.
I felt hot, my heart was racing,
and I could not focus.
It was a terrible experience.
From what I've heard, and what I've read;
that was anxiety.
That was the first time, I've ever felt that,
at least to that degree.
It truly helped me to understand those
who may suffer from anxiety.
So this chapter is for you.
I have met several people in my life
that experience this on a regular basis.
Maybe I had to feel that, to understand
them better.
And believe me it worked, and I do.

# WHEN IT WAS WRITTEN

# ANXIOUS MOMENTS

My anxiety
creeps inside of me
makes it hard to see
is this really me?
my thoughts are deceived
its harder to breathe
heat takes over me
whys this have to be?
my anxiety

# WAIT

Sometimes its hard to wait
to learn to be patient, and calm
anxiety takes over
and I begin to worry
then I remember God is in control...
things happen in His time, not mine
and so I wait
and I learn
then I find peace in the fact that
God is in control...
As the worry melts away
anxiety loosens its grip
and I continue to learn
and I continue to wait
things happen as they should
when I wait, and I remember
God is in control...

# ON EDGE

When my anxiety
creeps inside of me
and grabs ahold of me
I get all sweaty
and just start to worry

Tired of being on edge
my muscles are so tense
I'm exhausted but can not rest
irritable, and discontent

When my anxiety
creeps inside of me
nothings what it seems to be
so tired but can not sleep

Tired of being on edge
I'm cold, and trembling
my head is splitting
my stomach is in knots
and nothings what it seems to be

# CHAPTER 3

# AUTISM

Mark 10:14b

Suffer the little children to come unto me, and forbid them not; for of such is the kingdom of God.

KJV

This may be the least understood by me, and possibly others.

I do know that it is very wide spread, and very common.

It affects so many people in so many ways.

It also seems that many people who experience this condition have very strong talents, and abilities in many areas.

My hope is that you all find your special talent, your gift. And share that gift with the world.

We need you...

# WHEN IT WAS WRITTEN

# IF I CHOOSE

I'll take you on a trip inside my mind
you won't need a ticket
It is free entrance, if I choose.
You'll see all the pretty colors
and hear my sounds surround you
You will see things through my eyes
and yes, think my thoughts
Along the way, you will feel what I feel
It is free entrance, if I choose.
We will share space and time
my dreams, will be your dreams
my desires, your desires
you won't need a ticket
you can take this trip without leaving ground
It is free entrance, if I choose.

# FRUSTRATED

I'm frustrated
I don't know why
I want to scream
I want to cry
The tears won't come
My eyes are dry
I want to run
Wish I could fly
I feel so low
Wish I was high
What can I do?
What can I try?
I'm frustrated
I don't know why
I have to stop
I have to try
To search myself
To find out why
I know the truth
I can not lie
If I use, I'll surely die
I'm frustrated
I don't know why

# LIKE A BOOK

If my mind was a book
and I opened it to you

would you read a page?
could you read a chapter?
If you could read my mind
and it read like a book
would you understand?

If my mind was a book
and I opened it to you

I could hide nothing from you
it would be open
for you to know all
would you understand?

could you separate fantasy from reality?
would you see what was real?

If my mind was a book
and I opened it to you

would you accept me?
if you knew all
could you love me?
if you knew all.

If my mind was a book
and I opened it to you

For you to know all
would you love me?
If you knew all.

# CHAPTER 4

# BIPOLAR

Proverbs 3:5

Trust in the Lord with all thine heart; and lean not unto thine own understanding.

KJV

I may identify more with this diagnosis than many of the others. I experience the ups and downs in life like many others do.

I am greatful that the highs are not as high, and the lows are not as low as they were in the past.

But they definitly still exist.

Life is like a roller coaster that I used to want to get off. Now I enjoy the ride.

Not all days are easy, but I find peace in the fact that God is in control.

And where ever I am in my daily journey,

He is there with me.

# WHEN IT WAS WRITTEN

# BALANCE

The sky may be cloudy
The day may be gray
I choose to see beauty
The tenderness of the flower pedal
Though the root is strong
Always two sides to every coin
its sometimes unclear
But balance seems fair.
Times of pain easily forgotten
when joy surrounds us
and all is fine
Sometimes we give
and other times we receive
love is always near
if we are willing
all is not lost
when we open our minds
anything is possible
and balance seems fair.

# MY DISGUISE

I want to show you the real me
time to take off my disguise.
to do this I must face the truth
and look at myself in the eyes

What do I see when I search within?
who is that person inside?
Sometimes I feel like I wanna laugh
and sometimes I just wanna cry

I'm starting to feel some emotions
but my eyes they still are dry
I believe that this is all normal
when I decide to give it a try

At times I'd rather not go there
but I have to
take off my disguise.

# AS TWO WORLDS COLLIDE

I open my eyes as two worlds collide...
and pain and fear never subside
up the ladder its time to climb
to tell the truth, to tell the lie
to choose to live, to choose to die
I close my eyes as two worlds collide...
and evil, and darkness deep inside
within myself these things I hide
To search myself, to what I find
To cleanse my soul, to change my mind
I open my eyes as two worlds collide...
and hope, and peace, can they be mine?
I pray to my God, to Him I confide
The days in the past, the times that I've tried
The battle within, the thing I must fight
Thier is always a choice, as two worlds collide...

# CHAPTER 5

# BORDERLINE PERSONALITY DISORDER

Psalms 28:7

The Lord is my strength and my shield; my heart trusted in Him, and I am helped: therefore my heart greatly rejoiceth; and with my song will I praise Him.

KJV

I highly relate to this one as well. It describes many of my feelings, and it also helps me to see how, and why several things may have happened in my life, and my relationships over the years.

The symptoms, and characteristics so closely define me.

I actually wrote a new poem yesterday as I did some research.

It is titled Fear of Abandonment.

It is one of the biggest symptoms I personally deal with still to this day.

I am including that poem in this chapter

# WHEN IT WAS WRITTEN

# LOST WITHOUT YOU

I'm lost without you
I'm crushed without you
Watching you go, is so hard
Now I sit here, without you
I wish I could make it right
What I did wrong
But, its too late
and its so hard
being here without you
I wish I could fix
what I have broken
And, I'm crushed without you
I need you to see
I'm lost without you

# TANGLED WEB

I look back, its hard to believe
what a tangled web I weaved
The lie, its there to only decieve
I closed my eyes but could not sleep
because of the tangled web I weaved
when at times I fed my disease
It took all I had, I could not breathe
And now its time to find reprieve
when to stay, when to leave
when to feel joy, when to grieve
what a tangled web I weaved
woven so thick I could not see
I didn't know how to feel, or be
To stop the pain, to make is cease
what a tangled web I weaved
Now I give it to God, in Him I believe
To tear it apart, piece by piece

# FEAR OF ABANDONMENT

It terrifies me that you will leave
but I continue to feed my disease
why do I have such low self-esteem?
I push you away, but its you that I need
Self sabatage, I'm my worst enemy
Can't really control my mood swings
Please don't leave, its you that I need
Do I really exist? Am I me?
So I self sabatage, I feed my disease
For some reason, I can't escape my insecurities
And, it terrifies me that you will leave

# CHAPTER 6

## DEPRESSION

Matthew 11:28

Come unto me, all ye that labour and are heavy laden, and I will give you rest.

KJV

Like so many things in life, depression probably has many different levels, and forms based on the individual person, and what situations are going on for that person at that moment in time.

I experience this in small doses at different times.

It is way better than it used to be.

Because of the fact that I have dealt with many of my underlying issues.

Many of these thoughts, feelings, and emotions have all but left me.

I did a lot of work on myself, and my issues.

But I give God all the glory, and praise.

For without Him, I would still be stuck in a dark, empty place.

# WHEN IT WAS WRITTEN

I -     How I Feel, 2006

II -     Deep, Dark Place, 2021

III -     As Darkness Turns To Light, 2005

# HOW I FEEL

Do you know how I feel?
can you understand me?
I lived in fear so long
but now I have hope...
and I want to share with you
how I feel, my hope.
I lived in doubt so long
but now I have understanding...
I want to share with you
how I feel, my understanding.
Do you know how I feel?
I lived in a cage for so long
But now I have love...
And I want to share it with you
how I feel, my love.
I want to share with you
How I feel...

# DEEP, DARK PLACE

I feel I'm slipping into a
deep, dark place...
I need to find some light
in this place.

I need some help
to try to reclaim
lead me back to the light
from that darkness
where I came.

Show me just a glimpse
before its too late
you don't understand
all that's at stake.

I might be loosing myself
I may be slipping from grace
have you been sent here,
to show me the way?

To help me find some light
in this deep, dark place...

# AS DARKNESS TURNS TO LIGHT

As night turns into morning
and darkness turns to light
I have another opertunity
to choose to do what's right

I set aside a moment
to talk to God above
I thank Him for His grace
His faithfulness, His love

He gives me strength to do the things
that I must do today
to get through any obsticals
that might be in my way

Its nice to know that God is there
that I am not alone
as I continue on this journey
down this long, and winding road

As night turns into morning
and darkness turns to light
Each day I must surrender
I no longer have to fight

As hope turns into faith
my God is always near
Just knowing that I'm not alone
I no longer live in fear

Now anything is possible
my futures looking bright
each day now holds new meaning
as darkness turns to light.

# CHAPTER 7

## DISSOCIATIVE IDENITY DISORDER (DID)

Romans 8:38, 39

For I am persuaded, that neither death, nor life, nor angels, nor principalities, nor powers, nor things present, nor things to come.

Nor height, nor depth, nor any other creature, shall be able to seperate us from the love of God, which is in Christ Jesus our Lord.

KJV

When I read some of the symptoms associated with (DID) it reminded me of one of the rehabs I was in many years ago in my early 20s.

One of the daily activities was to look at the chart of different faces that described feelings.

☺ happy, ☹ sad, ??? angry, and so on.

To describe how we were feeling at that time.

I could not find my feeling on that chart.

So I came up with my own. It was like a balloon face on a long string, and I called it disconected ???.

I felt that way many times in my younger years.

And also the feeling of being detached from myself.

I rarely feel that anymore. But when I do, it reminds me from where I came, and to where I never want to return.

# WHEN IT WAS WRITTEN

I -     Disconnected, 2020

II -    Its Me, Its Not, 2021

III -   Flawed, 2020

# DISCONNECTED

The invisible cord
From the heart to the head

Mines disconnected
My feelings are dead

How did I end up
this way?

By the way I lived
by the choices I made

Sometimes I don't care
that's just the fact

Thankfully my spirit's
in tact.

My cords disconnected
I can not feel

So watch yours close
this stuff is real...

# ITS ME, ITS NOT

I should be fine
but I'm not
Is this mind mine?
It is, but its not
Something comes over me
not me, not myself
I should be fine
but I'm not
Please help me seperate
this, my mind
Its me, but its not

# FLAWED

Do you feel guilty for being flawed?
you are not broken,
when you fall short...
No one is perfect
there was only one...
Even though you are not fragile,
be gentle with you
practic forgiveness...
You are not broken,
but only flawed
Do not be sorry for this...
No one is perfect
there was only one...
You are not broken,
but only flawed...

# CHAPTER 8

# PANIC

2 Timothy 1:7

For God hath not given us the spirit of fear; but of power, and of love, and of a sound mind.

KJV

A full blown panic attack can be terrifying. I have had many, of what I would call small panic attacks.

They are called such for a very good reason.

I felt the attack on me physically, mentally, and even spiritually.

Different fears including -

The fear of not getting something I want, or the fear of losing something I have, and even bigger the fear of death, can easily be turned into a major panic episode.

In my personal journey, I would tend to turn these fears into anger.

For me anger was easier to relate to, and deal with than the actual fear itself.

This being said, I never really dealt with many of my fears. Thankfully God chose to remove them from me.

They were replaced with hope, and peace, and faith.

# WHEN IT WAS WRITTEN

# THIS NOISE

This noise in my head,
will not let me sleep.
Some of the scars,
go way too deep.
That if I was to share,
You'd say I was insane.
This noise in my head,
causes nothing but pain.
Why must I listen?
What can I do?
To open up,
To tell you the truth.
So what must I do,
to quiet this noise?
To have thoughts of love,
To have thoughts of joy.

This noise in my head,
not reality,
this noise in my head,
in sanity.
It won't let me sleep,
this noise in my head.
It won't let me rest,
This noise wants me dead.
So what must I do,
To silence this noise?
What must I do,
To take back my mind?
So I won't be afraid,
to close my eyes,
what must I do,
To take back my life?
I must find a way,
to silence this noise.

# 18

Are you demon possessed
or darkness obssessed???

The distance of 18 inches,
From your brain to your heart..

And 18 miles,
From your heart to your soul..

Will the light be brighter,
or the darkness grow??

Will you be carried by the light,
or dragged down below??

There's barely a flicker,
and the lights getting dim..

You must come to your senses,
You must run from him..

He's licking his fingers,
he's counting your sin...

# I AM AFRAID

My heart is frayed
I am afraid.
The games I played
choices I made
I must repay
all that I took away
I am afraid.
My heart is frayed
I need you Jesus
I believe
Forgive me Lord
These days, these nights
They all connect
This time I take
Time to reflect
I am afraid.
My heart is frayed
Forgive me Lord
My heart is frayed
I am afraid.

# CHAPTER 9

---

# PTSD
## (POSTRAMIC STRESS DISORDER)

Matthew 5:3

Blessed are the poor in spirt; for their's is the kingdom of heaven.

KJV

# WHEN IT WAS WRITTEN

This condition is often linked to our veterans, our brave soldiers, who experienced true war, and returned home with those scars, and memories. To you, I pause now, and I salute you. I can never repay you for what you did for me. This also touches many who were not in the military, or on the front lines.

Anyone who experienced, or witnessed a tramatic event can be affected, and deeply affected and changed for ever, if not helped.

Some of the worst may be those who were at literal war in thier own homes, and families.

Abuse comes in many forms.

If you are in danger please get help, and please get out.

You are worth so much.

You are allowed to be loved.

You are allowed to live in peace.

And most importantly, you are allowed to be you.

# DON'T CLOSE YOUR EYES

Don't close your eyes to the pain inside,
Everybody hurts, everybody cries.
We must learn to live this life,
through the pain, through the strife.
Share who we are, all the pain inside,
everybody hurts, everybody tries.
We only have so much time,
Your days are numbered, so are mine.
So don't close eyes to the love inside,
Share it with others, now is the time.
Keep your eyes open, don't be blind,
to all of the wonderful things in this life.
Everybody hurts, everybody dies.
So lets make the best of it,
And don't close your eyes.

# SCARS AND MEMORIES

Broken dreams
Fears, and worries
they all disapear in time
except our;
Scars and memories.
So many
thoughts and theries
and all that remains are
scars and memories.
From these we
Can not get away,
We can not escape,
We can not remove our
Scars and memories.

# NOTHING LEFT TO GIVE

If I give my heart freely
and you shred it to pieces
I have nothing left to give...

And with my broken heart
you crush my spirit
and all you do is take
I have nothing left to give...

Something must change...

And when you drown me of my energy
and my self control
and give nothing in return

You take bits, and pieces.
of me every time
until I have nothing left to give...

Something must change...
Something must give...

When you tear me down
and never build me up
and it feels like you drained
me of my very soul.

To the point that
I am an empty carcus
And I have nothing left to give...

Something must change...
Something must give...

# MERRY-GO ROUND

I was on a merry-go round
going round, and round
and I couldn't get off.
Going faster, radically out of control
afraid to jump, afraid to let go
to make the change, to take it slow.
To give of myself, instead of recieve.
To ask for help, to get on my knees..
to help someone else
to care for their needs.
Its that which I sow,
Its that which I reap..
gotta let go, gotta search deep
off the merry-go round, onto my feet.
Then I can help others, that also helps me.
To conquer my fears, to change what I see.
I gotta jump, I gotta let go
I can not reap, unless I sow
To give of myself, instead of receive
To reach out my hand, to help you believe.
I have faith in God, its trust I need
To get off the merry-go round onto my feet.

# CHAPTER 10

# SCHIZOPHRENIA

Proverbs 3:5

Trust in the Lord with all thine heart; and lean not unto thine own understanding.

I do remember experiencing many of the symptoms, thoughts, and feelings associated with this disorder.

And I also believe that they were in my case, drug induced.

So it is quite possibly seperate from the clinical diagnosis that many deal with throughout their lives.

It does in this way help me to understand some of what they, or you go through on a daily basis.

What I would like to say to you; is please continue in whatever is helping you.

This may include, but not be limited to counciling, medication, and therapy.

All too often people start feeling better, and choose to stop what they are doing, that is helping them.

This can be a grave mistake. God Bless You.

# WHEN IT WAS WRITTEN

# CRAWL

You may attempt
to infiltrate
But you can not
come within
you may creep
into my mind
but you cannot
crawl
in my skin

# EMPTY SHELL

I feel like something is wrong with me
like I am an empty shell.
As if someone reached deep
inside of me,
and ripped out my soul, or
even worse, something...

I lived the life I wanted to live,
and I payed a terrible price.
not many can pay this price.
and very few survive.
The symptoms, and the consequences
of being an empty shell.

A head full of angels and demons
a room full of saints and heathens
trying to take me to heaven, to hell.
and there I sit
a lonely, empty shell.

If I could change the way you see me,
and see that something is wrong.
This is not the way I wanted to live
is it too late for me to change?

A room full of saints and heathens
A head full of angels and demons.
So was this a choice I made?
or a choice made by someone,
or even worse something?

So am I a victim to this?
or did I truly survive?
am I dead? or am I alive?
the price is too high
is this heaven, or hell?
Here I sit
a lonely, empty shell.

# TORMENTING CONFLICTS

Broken in pieces
but, not torn apart
tormenting conflicts
ripped out my heart.
mental defects
physical aspects
social rejects
Broken in pieces
but, not torn apart

# CHAPTER 11

# SELF INJURY/CUTTING

I Corinthians 6:20

For ye are bought with a price; therefore glorify God in your body, and in your spirit, which are God's.

KJV

This is something I am all too familiar with. I experienced self injury in my early adult life; my early to late twenties.

Some of it I believe was an attempt to get some very much wanted, and needed attention.

I few things I remember hearing over time that it can be a distraction from painful emotions through physical pain.

It can be an expression of internal feelings in an external way.

I also believe that when I was feeling empty; it was my way of feeling something: ANYTHING.

All of these reasons were real, but they did not help at all.

In fact they made things worse.

Worsening feelings of shame, guilt, and low self esteem, and many other underlying feelings

# WHEN IT WAS WRITTEN

I -    Sweet Catastrophy, 2020

II -    Cut, 2006

III -    Mistake, 2021

# SWEET CATASTROPHY

Why did he slip, rip?
Why was his wrist slit?

He was a product of the system
a sweet catastrophy.

Everyone looked, but
no one could see...

Why didn't he tell you?
he tried.

The times he opened up
and cried.

Everyone looked, but
no one could see ...

He was a product of the system
a sweet catastrophy.

# CUT

as the blood flows through the vein
and the cut releases pain...
and the cloud becomes rain
then I know the angels cry
and a seed becomes a bloom
and a spark becomes a flame
as if its just a game
nothing is the same
and everything will change
in a moment I'm insane
when I cut against the grain
and all my fluids drained
the angels cry, it rains
and the cut releases pain...

# MISTAKE

All the mistakes you made
staring at the sharp blade
please remember things can change
I can help you.
Every choice you make
every cut you chase
every scar you claim
please let me help you.
You are not a mistake...

# "BROKEN"

Wow, so on that journey I took trying to compile my information for this book, I had so many thoughts, and memories concerning me, and my mental health over my lifetime. It also made me think of so many others.

Their are many different definitions, and lists of symptoms, and behaviors for each category I chose to write on.

Not everyone agrees on these, so I chose to just talk about me, my experiences.

If you can relate to any of them, my hopes would be that you looked more into it.

Their is much help for us out there.

So please realize that you are not alone, and like in the opening statements of this book. It is very important that I repeat it.

My mental health, and my recovery go hand in hand.

We must treat them both in order to have reprieve. And we cannot do it alone.

In my personal story, I am so greatful for all of my experiences in life, every thing I went through, and continue to go through in this life brings me closer to God, and ultimately closer to me. Which in turn brings me closer to you.

We are social by nature. God made us that way.

We need each other.

Like a chain has many links, and in that chain, if one of those links is missing, or "broken", the chain looses it strength, and its purpose.

# CONCLUSION

In conclusion, I feel the need to say that in my opinion, and my opinion only.

I believe we are all "broken".

Its also my opinion that we, as humans quite possibly fall into one, or many of these categories; to some degree, that's what makes us human.

I'm not sure what the true definition for the word "normal" is.

Find some help if you need it. And remember you are not a mistake.

You are God's greatest creation, and God is incapable of making mistakes.

You are worth Good things.

You can be anything you want to be.

Seek God, and find yourself in the process.

We need Him, and each other,

One important, final statement:

Only you can be you...

Printed in the United States
by Baker & Taylor Publisher Services